I CAN MAKE IT!
I CAN READ IT!

20 Reproducible Booklets to Develop Early Literacy Skills

SPRING

WRITTEN BY:

Susan Bunyan, Susan DeRiso,
Lucia Kemp Henry, Suzanne Moore

EDITED BY:

Kim T. Griswell
Mackie Rhodes

ILLUSTRATED BY:

Pam Crane, Teresa R. Davidson, Theresa Lewis Goode, Sheila Krill,
Rob Mayworth, Greg D. Rieves, Rebecca Saunders,
Barry Slate, Donna K. Teal

COVER DESIGN BY:

Nick Greenwood and Kimberly Richard

©2000 by THE EDUCATION CENTER, INC.
All rights reserved.

ISBN# 1-56234-403-X

Manufactured in the United States
10 9 8 7 6 5 4 3 2 1

TABLE OF CONTENTS

RAINBOW COLORS

Rhyming text and colors so bright make this two-day booklet a rainbow delight! For each child, copy pages 4–6 on construction paper; then prepare four nine-inch paper plates as follows: cut four inches off the first plate, three inches off the second, and two inches off the last two (discard one of the two-inch sections). Set aside one seven-inch plate section. On the first day, each child paints the front of her plates in this order from largest to smallest: red, orange, yellow, green, blue, and purple. On the second day, she cuts out each pattern and colors as follows (pattern page 7 and the cloud pattern are left uncolored): the rose red, the orange orange, the sun yellow, the grass green, the eyes blue, the grapes purple, and the title a variety of colors.

To make booklet pages 1–6, the child glues each cutout near the straight edge of the plate corresponding to the picture color. For booklet page 7, she glues the text cutout to the curved edge of the other seven-inch plate section (front side) and then draws a picture of herself and a friend on the page. To make the cover, she writes her name on the title cutout and then glues it to the back of booklet page 1 as shown. Then she creates a rainbow by sequencing booklet pages 1–6 with the straight edges together. She tops booklet page 6 with the cloud cutout and places booklet page 7 facedown on top of the stack. Then she punches a hole through the pages and ties them together with ribbon. Invite each child to read her completed booklet to you. Point out the rainbow that appears as she flips each page. Beautiful!

Extend this activity by sharing Greg & Steve's "Rainbow of Colors" from *We All Live Together, Volume 5* (Youngheart Music, Inc.).

Red like roses that smell so sweet. 1

Orange like fruit, so good to eat. 2

Yellow like the sun on a bright warm day. 3

Green like the grass where I run and play. 4

Blue like the eyes of a friend of mine. 5

Purple like grapes that grow on the vine. 6

Put them together. What do you see? A rainbow of colors for you and me! 7

Rainbow Colors by Kim

Booklet Cover, Pattern, and Page

Use with "Rainbow Colors" on page 3.

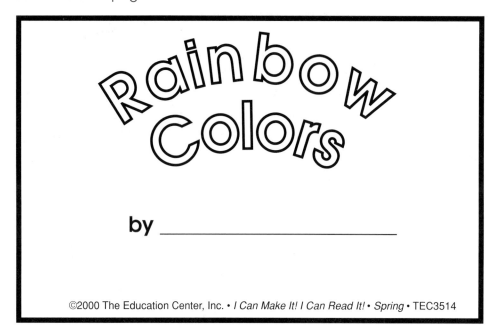

Rainbow Colors

by _____

cloud

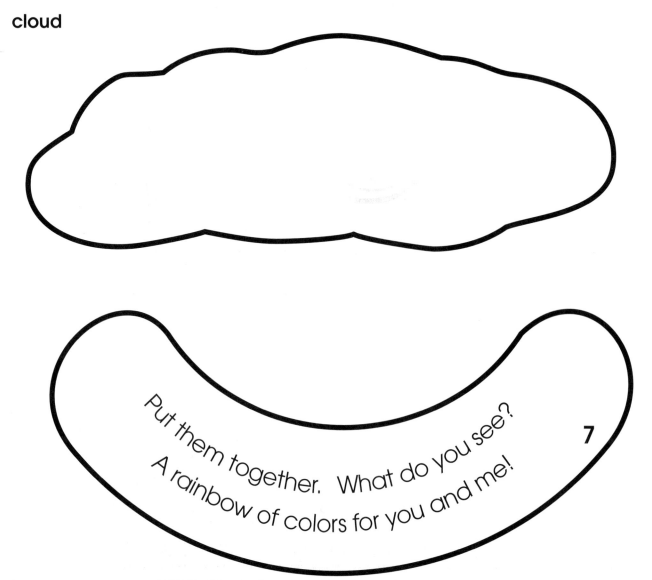

Put them together. What do you see?
A rainbow of colors for you and me!

7

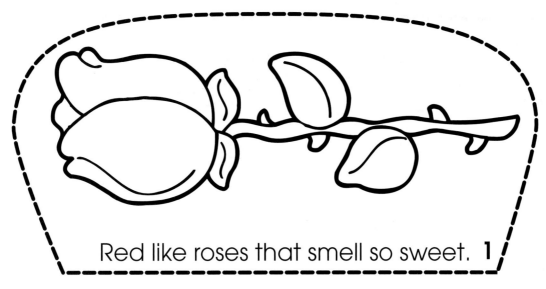

Red like roses that smell so sweet. **1**

Orange like fruit, so good to eat. **2**

Yellow like the sun on a bright warm day. **3**

Booklet Pages
Use with "Rainbow Colors" on page 3.

Green like the grass where I run and play. **4**

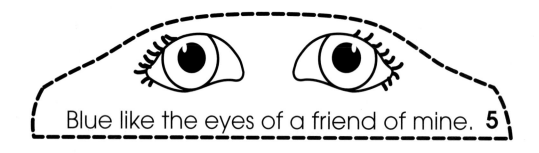

Blue like the eyes of a friend of mine. **5**

Purple like grapes that grow on the vine. **6**

A HEALTHY ME

Exercise youngsters' creativity as they learn about health with these cute booklets. To begin, duplicate pages 8–11 on white construction paper to make a class supply. Then instruct each child to cut out his booklet cover and pages. Have him complete each page according to the directions below. Afterward, help the child sequence his pages and then staple them behind the cover. Ask each child to read his booklet to a partner; then have him take it home to share with his family.

PAGE-DECORATING INSTRUCTIONS:

Cover: Write your name on the line. Color each picture.

Page 1: Color the soap with a light crayon color, applying firm pressure as you color. Paint the water with water-thinned blue tempera paint.

Page 2: Color the toothpaste tube. Color a craft stick with a crayon; then glue it on the dotted lines. Use cotton to dab a little toothpaste on the toothbrush bristles.

Page 3: Draw a picture of yourself enjoying your favorite outdoor exercise.

Page 4: Glue magazine cutouts of healthy foods on the page.

Page 5: Draw yourself asleep in the bed. Color the picture.

Page 6: Draw a self-portrait.

> To extend this activity, conduct a survey to discover which brand of bar soap is most popular in your students' homes. Duplicate the survey form (page 11) and send it home with each child. After students return their forms, graph the results and share the findings.

A Healthy Me
by Austin

Soap and water, **1**

toothbrush and toothpaste, **2**

fresh air and play, too, **3**

Good meals and snacks, **4**

plenty of sleep, **5**

are healthy for me. It's true! **6**

Dear Family,
What brand of bar soap is the most popular? Our class is taking a survey to find out! Please help your child write the name of your family's soap brand on the line. Then return this form by **Tuesday, March 14**
(date)

SOAP

Spring

A Healthy Me

by

_____

Soap and water,

1

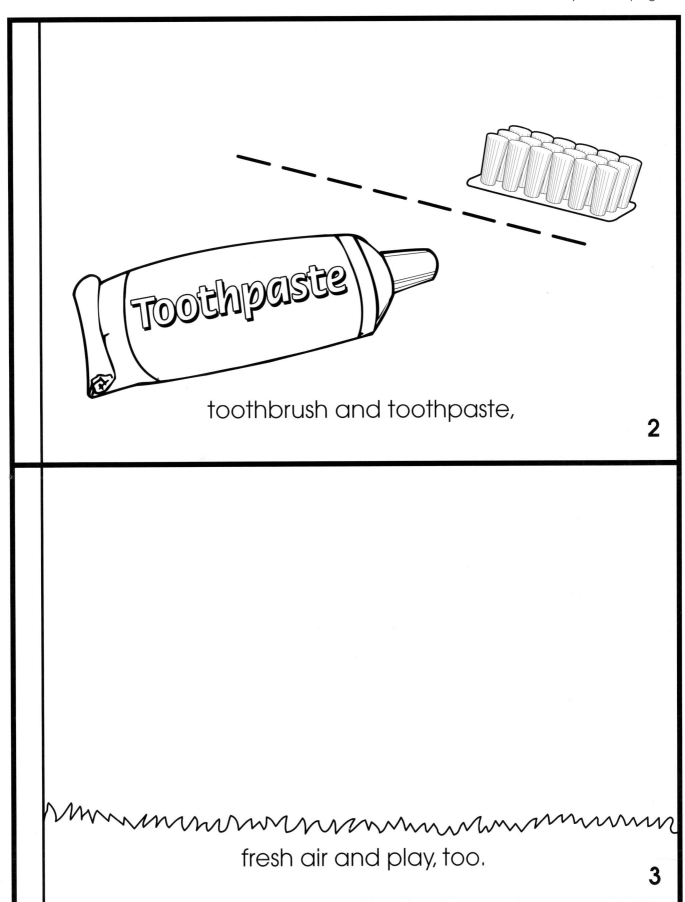

toothbrush and toothpaste,

2

fresh air and play, too.

3

Booklet Pages
Use with "A Healthy Me" on page 7.

Good meals and snacks,   4

plenty of sleep,   5

are healthy for me. It's true!

6

Dear Family,
What brand of bar soap is the most popular? Our class is taking a survey to find out! Please help your child write the name of your family's soap brand on the line. Then return this form by

_____.

(date)

_____

(soap brand)

UP, UP, AND AWAY!

Breeze into positional concepts with this high-flying booklet. To begin, duplicate pages 13–16 on white construction paper to make a class supply. Have each child color and cut out the booklet cover, pages, and kite pattern; then have her write her name on the cover. Help her cut the slits where indicated on booklet pages 1 and 6. Then ask the child to sequence and staple her pages behind the cover. To make the kite manipulative, have the child glue a six-inch-long ribbon tail to the cutout and then glue the resulting kite to a craft stick. Instruct her to store her kite in the slit on page 1. After all the booklets are completed, read them together as a class. Invite each child to remove her kite and manipulate it according to the text on each page. Later encourage your young kite fliers to share their booklets with family members. These booklets are sure to stir up a whirlwind of smiles and compliments!

To extend this activity, take your little investigators outside to look for evidence of the wind. Invite them to float feathers, small pieces of tissue paper, or even bubbles on the wind to determine its direction and strength.

Up, Up, and Away! by Hannah

Off the ground. Up, up, and away!

Beside the bee. Up, up, and away! 2

Under the birds. Up, up, and away! 3

Between the squirrels. Up, up, and away! 4

Over the house. Up, up, and away! 5

In the tree. Here to stay. 6

Up, Up, and Away!

by _____

Off the ground.
Up, up, and away!

1

©2000 The Education Center, Inc. • *I Can Make It! I Can Read It!* • *Spring* • TEC3514

Booklet Pages

Use with "Up, Up, and Away!" on page 12.

3

Under the birds.
Up, up, and away!

2

Beside the bee.
Up, up, and away!

5

Over the house.
Up, up, and away!

4

Between the squirrels.
Up, up, and away!

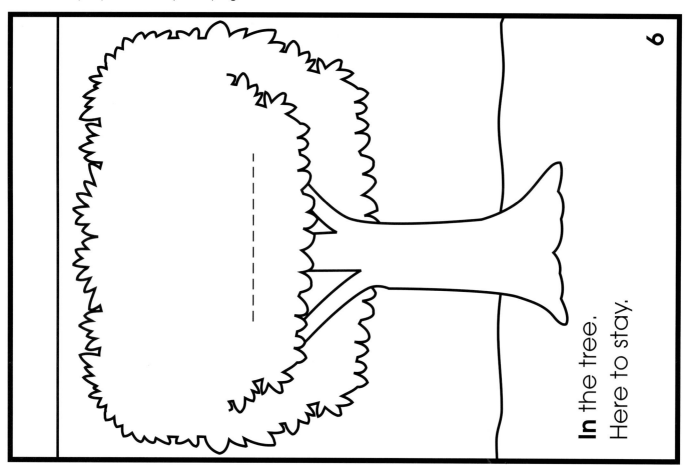

6

In the tree.
Here to stay.

kite

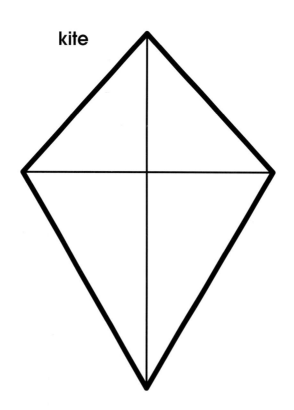

PINK PIG PACKS

This perky little pig packs a backpack, plays a flute, paints a picture, and plays peekaboo! For each child, duplicate the booklet cover, pages, patterns, and backing (pages 18–20) on white construction paper. Ask each child to color the pig body pink in each picture. Then have him cut out the booklet pages and patterns. Instruct the child to decorate each page according to the instructions below. When his pages are completed, have him sequence them and staple them to the backing where indicated. Then invite pairs of students to read their alliterative pig tales together.

PAGE-DECORATING INSTRUCTIONS:

Cover: Draw a few items inside the backpack. Write your name on the flap cutout; then color the backpack and flap to match. Staple the flap to the cover where indicated.

Page 1: Color the flute cutout. Glue it to the page where indicated.

Page 2: Draw a picture on the rectangle to represent a painting.

Backing: Color the arm cutouts pink. Use a brad to attach each arm to the pig's body where indicated.

> Extend this activity by prompting your party of little people to brainstorm a list of action words that begin with *P*, such as *pull*, *push*, and *pound*. Write their responses on a large pink pig cutout; then invite students to act out each word.

Pink Pig Packs

Staple flap here.

©2000 The Education Center, Inc. • *I Can Make It! I Can Read It!* • *Spring* • TEC3514

Pink Pig Plays.

Glue flute here.

1

©2000 The Education Center, Inc. • *I Can Make It! I Can Read It!* • *Spring* • TEC3514

Pink Pig paints.

flute

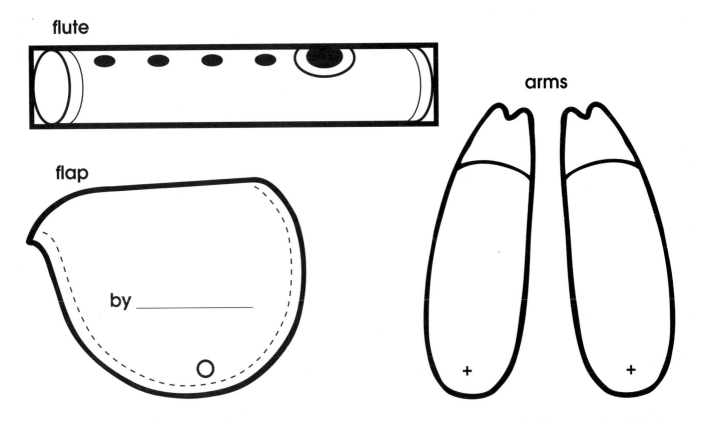

arms

flap

by _____

Pink Pig peeks!

Staple pages here.

SEEDS

Use this lift-the-flap booklet to teach youngsters about gardening. For each child you will need a pumpkin, sunflower, tomato, and green bean seed, as well as five sheets of yellow construction paper and a green pipe cleaner. Copy four green construction paper leaf patterns and four brown construction paper pot patterns (page 22) for each child. Then copy the remaining patterns (page 22) and pages 23–26 on white paper to make a class supply.

To make a booklet, each child colors and cuts out her white pages and patterns. She glues each page onto a sheet of yellow paper and then glues the corresponding seed onto each page. To make the flaps, the child glues a pot where indicated on each page. Next, she writes her name on the title cutout and glues it to the last sheet of yellow paper. Then she tears each seed packet to resemble an open pack of seeds and then glues it on the cover. To assemble her booklet, the child sequences the pages, punches two holes along the left edge, and twists a green pipe cleaner half (stem) through each set of holes. Finally, she punches a hole in each leaf, attaches two leaves to each pipe cleaner stem, twists, and then curls the stems around a pencil. Read these booklets together, inviting youngsters to lift the flaps to discover the surprise in each pot. Then encourage students to share their garden treasures with their families.

To enhance this activity, invite each child to plant a bean seed in a cup of soil. Then encourage her to tend to her plant as she observes its magical growth.

21

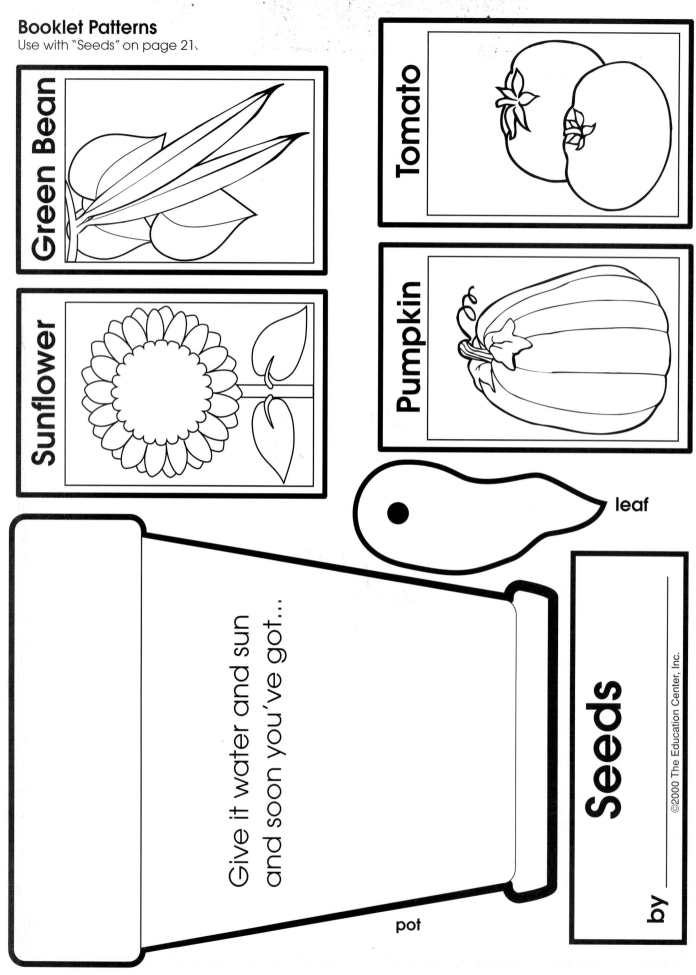

Green Bean

Tomato

Sunflower

Pumpkin

leaf

Give it water and sun and soon you've got...

pot

Seeds

by

©2000 The Education Center, Inc.

Add this seed to soil in a pot.

x

a pumpkin plant
growing in your pot!

Glue pot here.

1

Use with "Seeds" on page 21.

Add this seed to soil in a pot.

X

a sunflower plant
growing in your pot!

Glue pot here.

2

Add this seed to soil in a pot.

x

a tomato plant
growing in your pot!

Glue pot here.

3

Add this seed to soil in a pot.

x

a green bean plant
growing in your pot!

Glue pot here.

4

IT'S RAINING!

Create a downpour of reading excitement for your puddle jumpers with these easy-to-read booklets. To prepare, locate a small photo of each child. Then duplicate pages 28–30 on white construction paper to make a class supply. Ask each child to cut out his booklet cover and pages; then help him cut out the opening on booklet page 5. Have him follow the directions below to decorate each page. Afterward, help the child sequence his pages and staple them together behind the cover. Send each child home with his booklet to share with his family.

PAGE-DECORATING INSTRUCTIONS:

Cover: Write your name on the line. Color the cloud gray; then glue wisps of cotton around its edges. Glue blue rice raindrops under the cloud.

Page 1: Draw a handle; then paint the umbrella with your choice of glue paint.

Page 2: Paint the raincoat with a light color of glue paint.

Page 3: Color the hat with a glitter crayon.

Page 4: Color the boots.

Page 5: Back the opening with your picture. Color each piece of rainwear to match its picture on a previous page.

> To extend this activity, determine which raincoat color is most popular in your classroom. On a rainy day, have youngsters don their raincoats. Record the raincoat colors on a graph; then share the results.

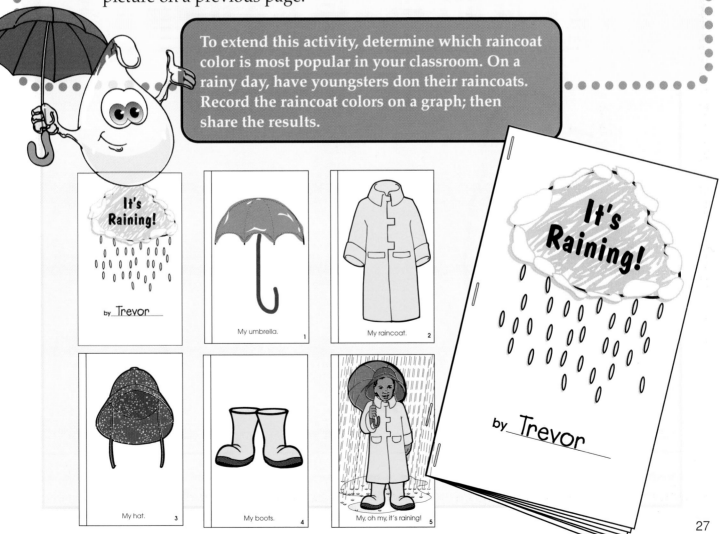

Booklet Cover and Page
Use with "It's Raining!" on page 27.

My umbrella.

1

It's Raining!

by _____

3

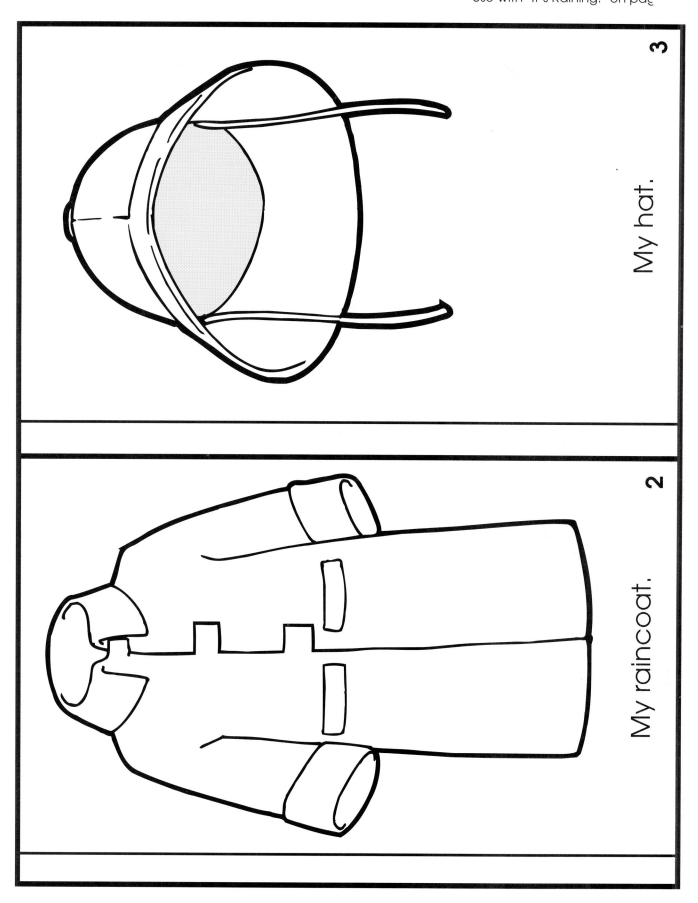

My hat.

2

My raincoat.

Booklet Pages

Use with "It's Raining!" on page 27.

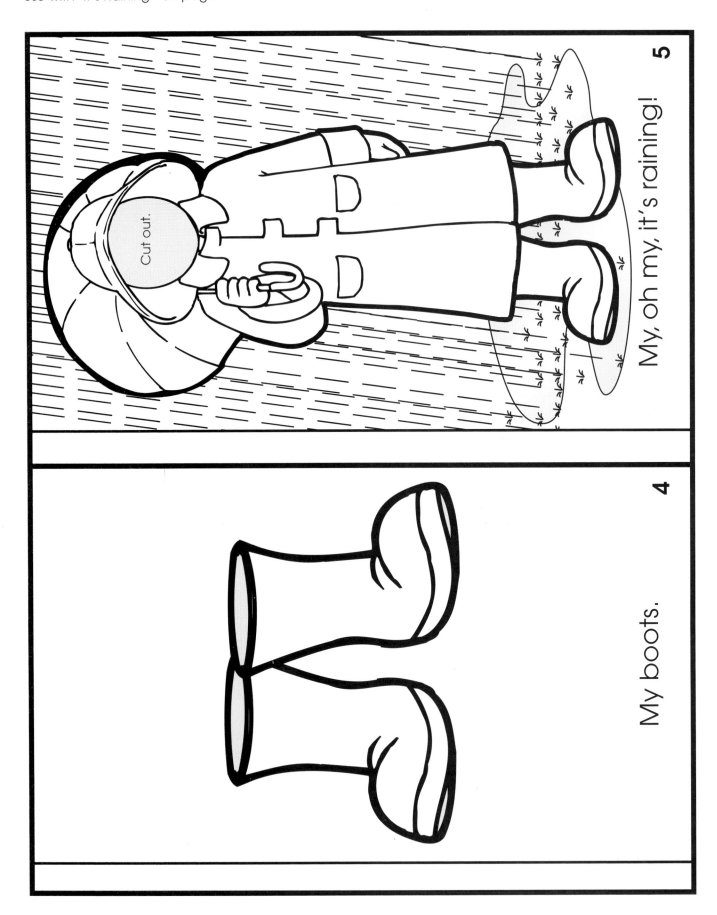

5

Cut out.

My, oh my, it's raining!

4

My boots.

THE POND

Take youngsters on a wetlands adventure through the pages of these booklets. Copy the booklet cover (page 32) on light green paper, the booklet page (page 33) on light blue paper, the flower patterns (page 34) on pink paper, and the remaining patterns (pages 32–34) on white paper to make a class supply. Then mask the text on the booklet page and copy it five times on light blue paper for each child. Have each child cut out her cover, pages, and patterns and then color her white patterns. Ask her to glue a text box to each blank page; then have her follow the directions below to complete each page. Afterward, help her sequence her pages and then staple them together at the top. Then invite student partners to share their booklets.

PAGE-DECORATING INSTRUCTIONS:

Cover: Write your name on the line. Glue the large flower on the cover where indicated; then glue the small flower on top of it.

Page 1: Draw waves on the page. Glue on a few strands of Easter grass.

Page 2: Glue the small end of the fin to the fish where indicated. Glue the fish on the page.

Page 3: Glue the dragonfly on the page. Line the wings with glitter.

Page 4: Cut a four-inch horizontal slit through the page. Attach the duck to the page with a brad as shown.

Page 5: Glue the frog to the page; then add wiggle eyes. Accordion-fold each leg. Glue one end of each leg to the frog where indicated. Then glue a foot to the loose end of each leg.

Page 6: Glue the turtle on the page; then glue brown paper squares on its shell.

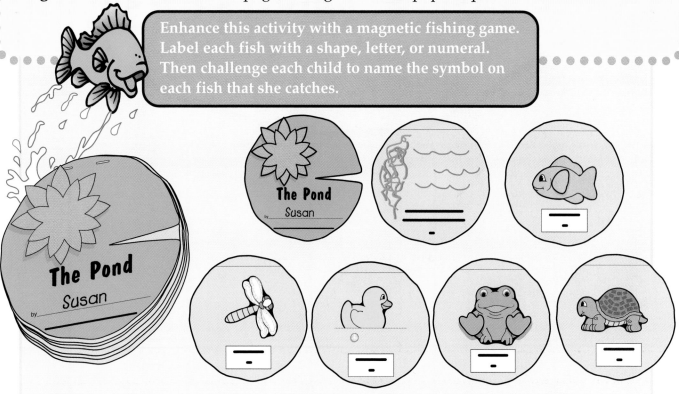

Enhance this activity with a magnetic fishing game. Label each fish with a shape, letter, or numeral. Then challenge each child to name the symbol on each fish that she catches.

Booklet Cover and Text Boxes

Use with "The Pond" on page 31.

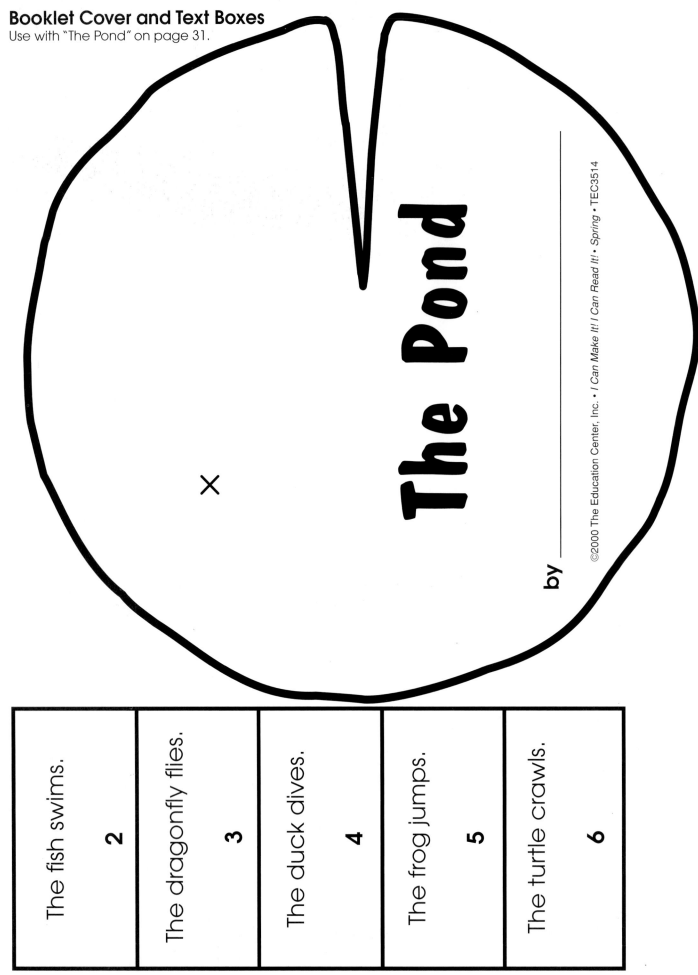

The Pond

by _____

The fish swims.

2

The dragonfly flies.

3

The duck dives.

4

The frog jumps.

5

The turtle crawls.

6

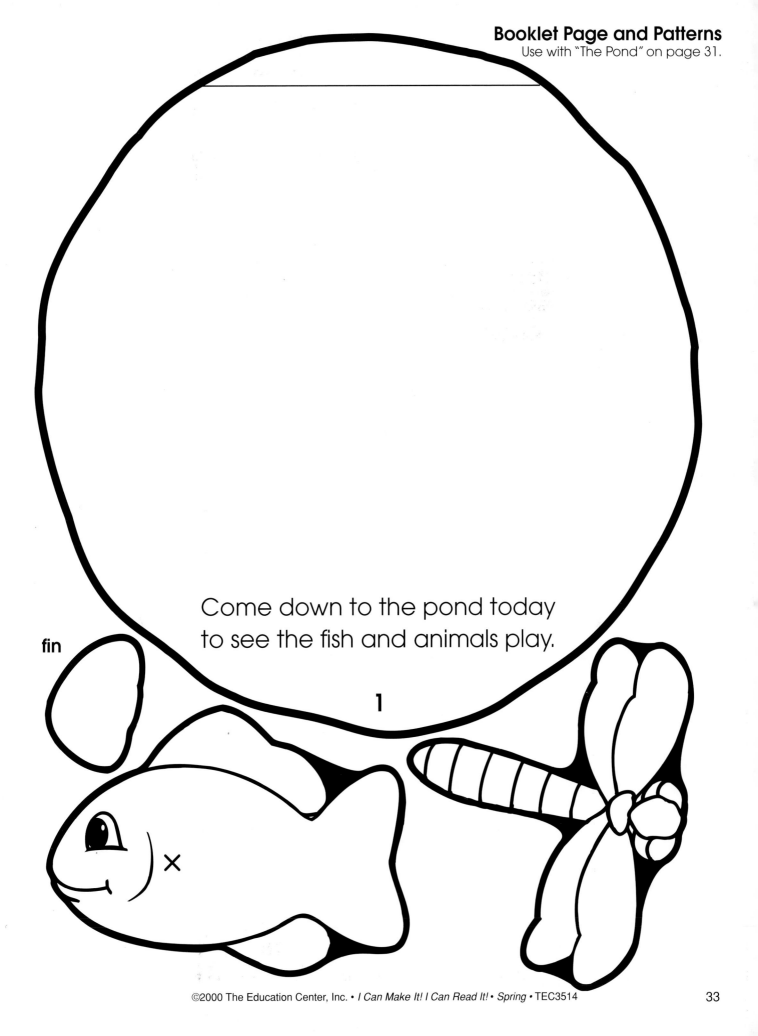

fin

Come down to the pond today
to see the fish and animals play.

1

Booklet Patterns

Use with "The Pond" on page 31.

feet

legs

flowers

WHAT'S IN THE EGG?

Youngsters will delight in cracking open the pages of these "eggs-citing" booklets. For each child, cut one 6" x 7" sheet and four 6" x 12" sheets of yellow construction paper. Also copy the text box and the two egg patterns (page 36) four times for each child. Then copy the cover (page 36) and the booklet pages (pages 37–38) on white construction paper to make a class supply.

To make a booklet, each child cuts out his booklet pages and patterns. He colors the picture on each page. Then he uses a brad to attach an egg top and bottom to each page as shown. To make a pocket for each egg, the child folds up five inches on each long sheet of yellow paper and staples the side edges together. Then he glues a text box to the front of each pocket. The child writes a different numeral from 1–4 on each pocket. He inserts each egg into the corresponding pocket. To make a cover, the child writes his name on the line. Then he glues the cover to the small sheet of yellow paper. Finally, he sequences his pockets behind the cover, punches two holes along the left edge, and ties the pocket together with ribbon. When his booklet is completed, encourage each child to crack it open and read it to a loved one.

Enhance this activity with an "eggs-ceptional" guessing game. For each child, secretly place a small item in a plastic egg. Invite him to explore the egg without opening it to try to guess its contents. Also give him clues to help him guess. Then have the child open the egg to check his answer.

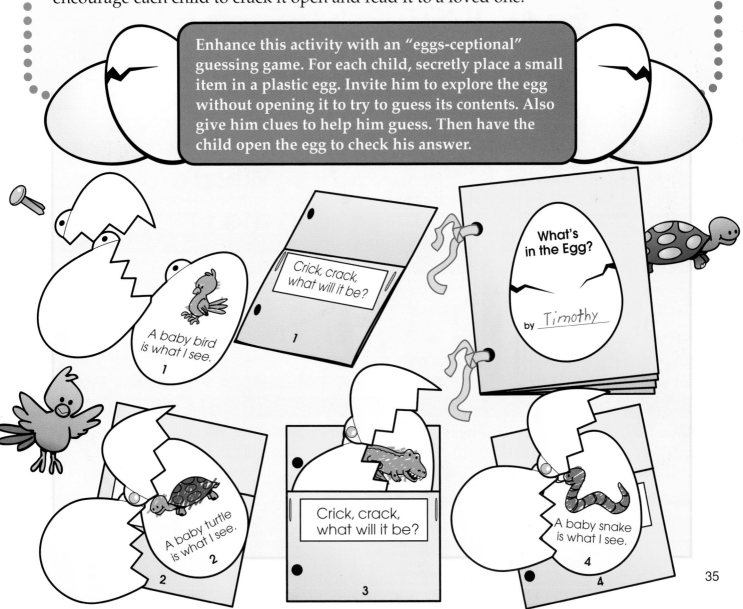

Crick, crack, what will it be?

A baby bird is what I see. 1

What's in the Egg?

by Timothy

A baby turtle is what I see. 2

Crick, crack, what will it be?

A baby snake is what I see. 4

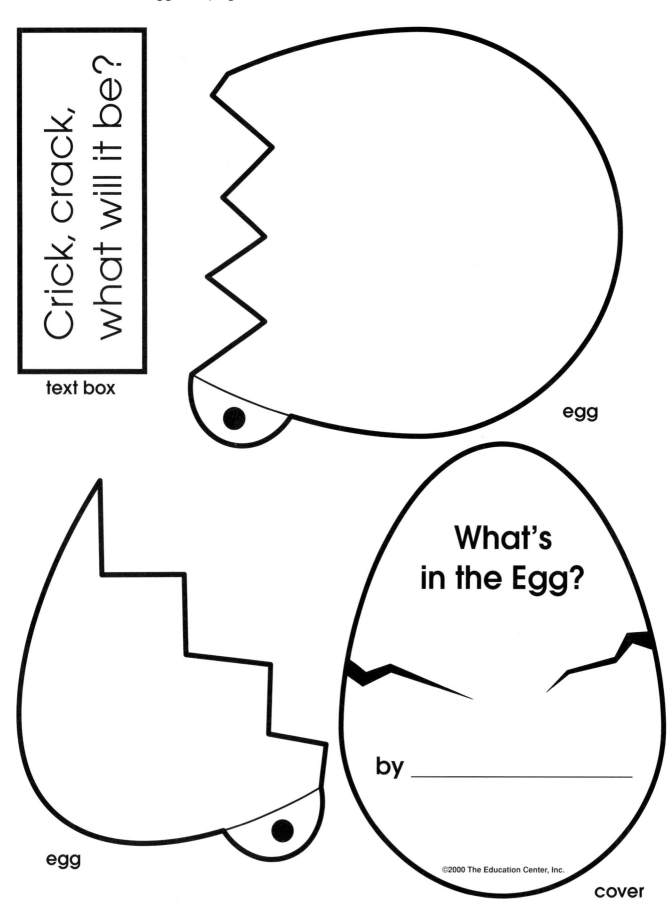

Crick, crack, what will it be?

text box

egg

egg

What's
in the Egg?

by _____

©2000 The Education Center, Inc.

cover

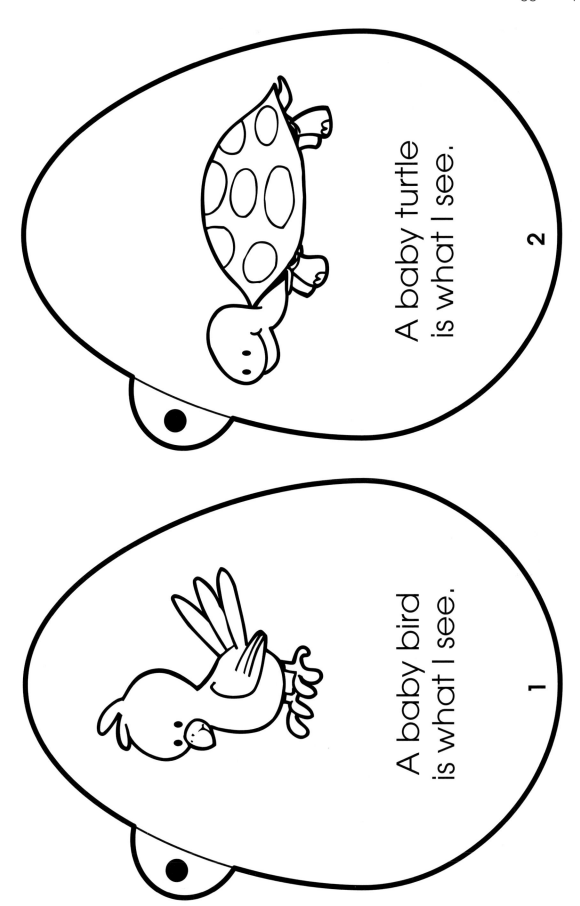

A baby turtle
is what I see.

2

A baby bird
is what I see.

1

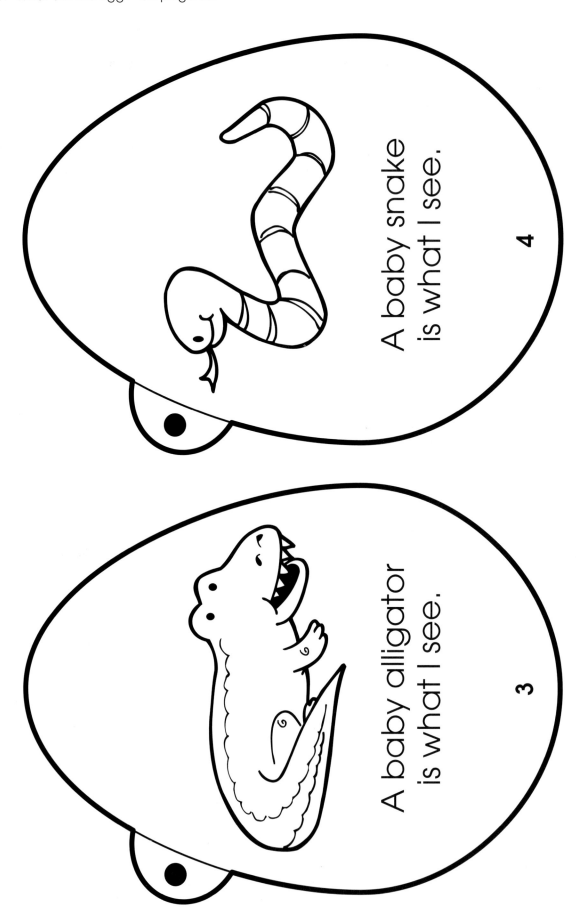

A baby snake
is what I see.

4

A baby alligator
is what I see.

3

©2000 The Education Center, Inc. • *I Can Make It! I Can Read It!* • *Spring* • TEC3514

WHAT DOES BUNNY DO?

Who's that hopping down the bunny trail? Why, it's a lively little rabbit that wiggles, twitches, and thumps along the way! To make these booklets, copy pages 40–43 on white construction paper to make a class supply. Then ask each child to color and cut out her booklet cover, pages, and patterns. Have her decorate the pages according to the instructions below. Once the pages are completed, help the child sequence them and staple them to the cover. Then read the booklets with small groups of students. Encourage each child to manipulate the bunny part as described on each page. Later, invite her to hippity-hop home to share her booklet with her family.

PAGE-DECORATING INSTRUCTIONS:

Cover: Glue the rabbit cutout to the cover. Write your name on the line.
Page 1: Glue a small ball of pink tissue paper (or a pom-pom) to the bunny's nose.
Page 2: Glue one end of three black paper strips to the side of the bunny's nose.
Page 3: Use a brad to attach the ear cutout to the page where indicated.
Page 4: Use a brad to attach the foot cutout to the page where indicated.
Page 5: Glue a small piece of cotton to the bunny's tail.
Page 6: Glue the egg basket to the bunny's arm.

To extend this activity, invite youngsters to create large paintings of bunnies. Label a separate sentence strip with each action word from the story, as well as student-generated words. Then display the paintings and labels with the title "What Do Bunnies Do?"

What Does Bunny Do?

by Peta

Bunny wiggles his nose.

Bunny twitches his whiskers.

Bunny flops his ear.

Bunny thumps his foot.

Bunny fluffs his tail.

Bunny does the Bunny Hop!

What Does Bunny Do?

by _____

Bunny wiggles his nose.

1

2

Bunny twitches his whiskers.

3

Bunny flops his ear.

4

Bunny thumps his foot.

5

Bunny fluffs his tail.

Bunny does the Bunny Hop!

9

ear

foot

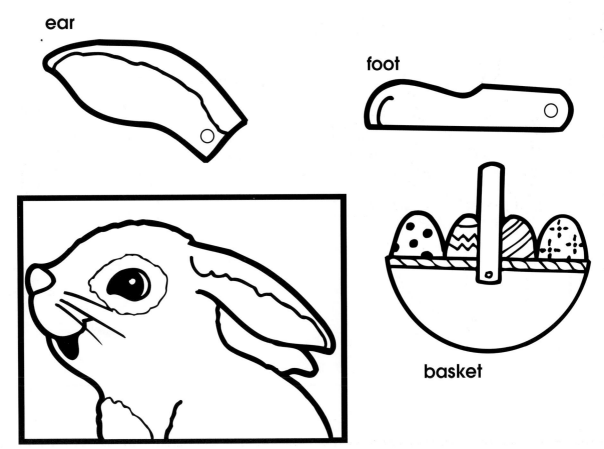

basket

THAT'S MY PLAN

During your Earth Day celebration, inspire little ones to think "recycle" with these lift-the-flap booklets. To prepare, gather some newspaper and a supply of magazines and grocery store flyers that picture lots of food containers. Then duplicate pages 45–48 on white construction paper to make a class supply. Ask each child to color and cut out his booklet pages and recycling bin patterns. Then have him follow the directions below to decorate each page. Afterward, help the child glue each lid cutout where indicated on the corresponding page. Then have him sequence his pages and staple them to the cover. Encourage your earth-friendly students to share their booklets with each other now and with their families later.

PAGE-DECORATING INSTRUCTIONS:

Cover: Write your name on the line.
Page 1: Glue small pieces of newspaper and other types of paper on the bin.
Page 2: Glue cutouts of plastic containers on the bin.
Page 3: Glue cutouts of cans on the bin.
Page 4: Glue cutouts of glass containers on the bin.

RECYCLE!

To extend this activity, invite youngsters to make recycling reminder necklaces. Have each child cut out a construction paper copy of the pattern (page 47) and then glue it to a yogurt lid. After the glue dries, help him poke a hole through the lid and thread a length of yarn through the hole.

I'll keep the earth as clean as I can.   1

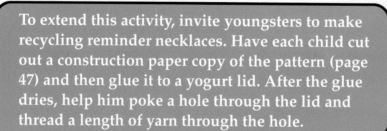

That's My Plan

by David

Recycle **glass.** That's my plan.

I'll keep the earth as clean as I can.   4

Recycle **plastic.** That's my plan.

I'll keep the earth as clean as I can.   2

Cola Cola   SOUP

I'll keep the earth as clean as I can.   3

That's
My Plan

by _____

Glue lid here.

I'll keep the earth as clean as I can.

1

Booklet Pages
Use with "That's My Plan" on page 44.

Glue lid here.

I'll keep the earth as clean as I can.

2

Glue lid here.

I'll keep the earth as clean as I can.

3

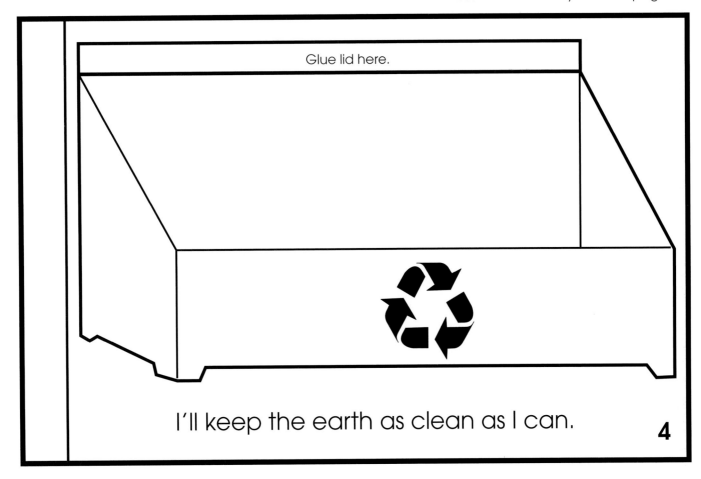

Glue lid here.

I'll keep the earth as clean as I can.

4

Recycle!
That's My
Plan

RECYCLE

Booklet Patterns
Use with "That's My Plan" on page 44.

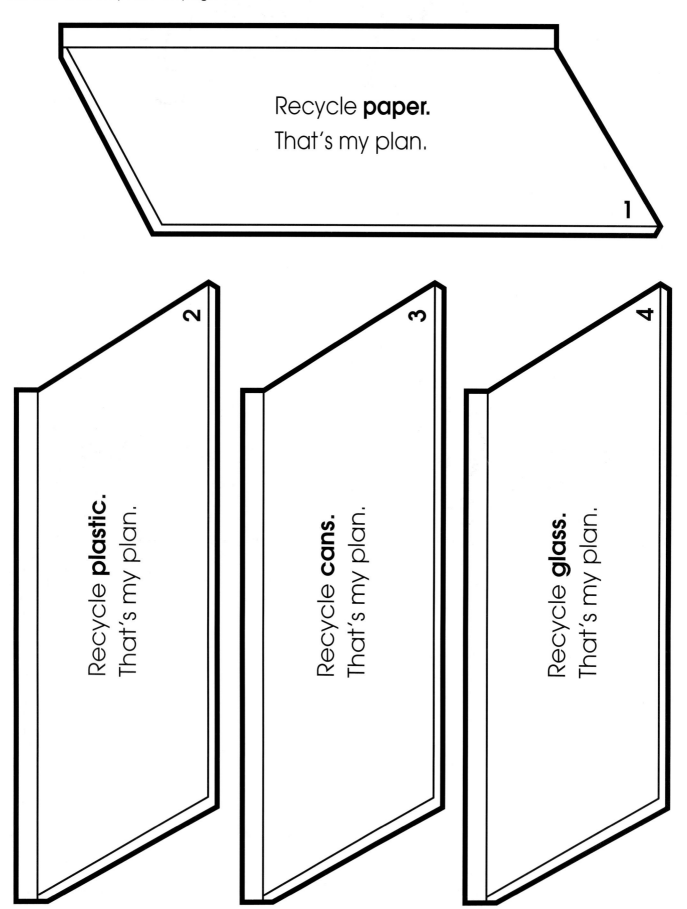

Recycle **paper.**
That's my plan.

1

2

Recycle **plastic.**
That's my plan.

3

Recycle **cans.**
That's my plan.

4

Recycle **glass.**
That's my plan.

LOOK ON A LEAF

Your class will go buggy over word-recognition skills with these insect-filled booklets. For each child, copy pages 50–52 on white construction paper and page 53 on light green construction paper. First, have each child cut out her booklet cover, pages, word wheel, and backing. Then help her cut out the small window on her backing. Next, have the child color the cover green and write her name on the line. Then have her color the insect picture on each of pages 1–7. Ask her to draw a few insects on page 8; then have her draw her favorite insect on the backing. Help her write the insect's name on the line. Then have the child use a brad to attach the word wheel to the backing where indicated. Finally, direct her to sequence her cover and pages and staple them to the backing. During a choral reading of the booklets, challenge youngsters to find the word on the wheel that matches the insect name on each page. Then invite each child, in turn, to share her last page with the class.

To extend this activity, make insect sight word posters for your writing center. Color and cut out an enlarged copy of each insect picture from the booklet. Glue each cutout to a separate sheet of construction paper; then label each poster with the insect name. Encourage youngsters to refer to the posters during their creative-writing activities.

dragonfly

Look
on a Leaf

by Betsy

©2000 The Education Center, Inc.

Look! A **grasshopper** on a leaf. 1

Look! A **dragonfly** on a leaf. 2

Look! An **ant** on a leaf. 3

Look! A **butterfly** on a leaf.

butterfly

Look! A **caterpillar** on a leaf. 5

Look! A **firefly** on a leaf. 6

Look! A **ladybug** on a leaf. 7

Look! Lots of **insects** on a leaf. 8

Look! My favorite insect on a leaf.

49

Booklet Cover and Pages
Use with "Look on a Leaf" on page 49.

1

Look! A **grasshopper** on a leaf.

3

Look! An **ant** on a leaf.

Look
on a Leaf

by _____

2

Look! A **dragonfly** on a leaf.

5

Look! A **caterpillar** on a leaf.

7

Look! A **ladybug** on a leaf.

4

Look! A **butterfly** on a leaf.

6

Look! A **firefly** on a leaf.

Booklet Page and Wheel
Use with "Look on a Leaf" on page 49.

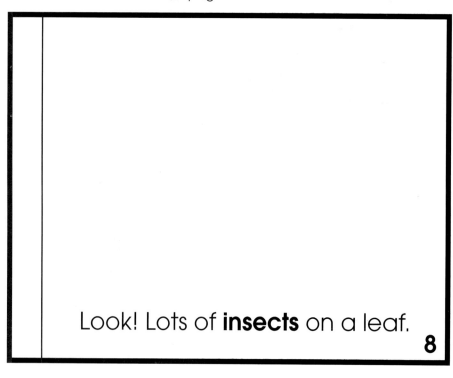

Look! Lots of **insects** on a leaf.

8

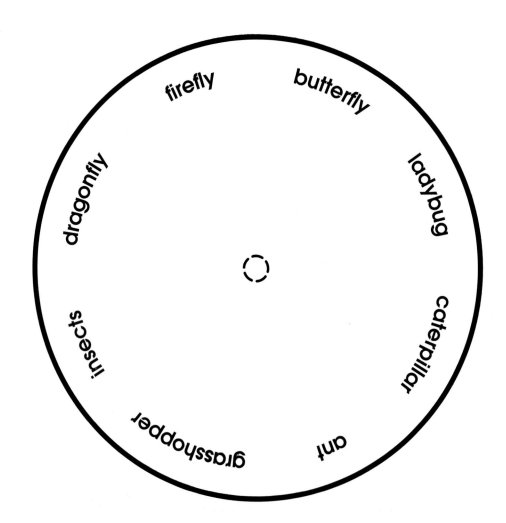

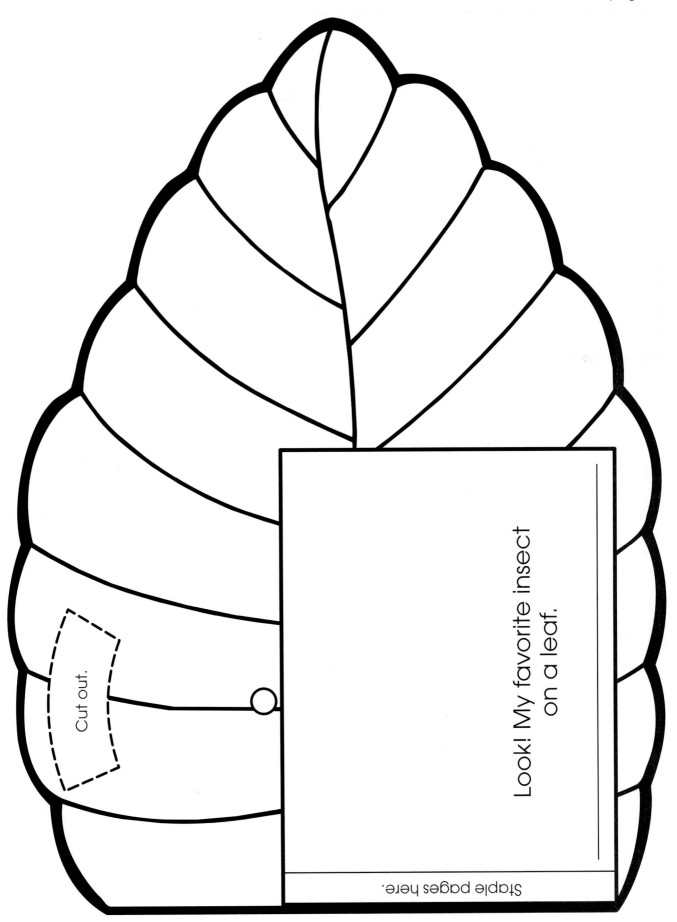

Cut out.

Look! My favorite insect on a leaf.

Staple pages here.

ANIMAL BABIES

Youngsters will enjoy repeated readings about their favorite baby animals with these very special picture albums. To begin, duplicate pages 55–57 on a light color of construction paper and page 58 on white construction paper to make a class supply. Then have each child color the animal puzzle patterns on page 58. Ask him to draw his favorite animal baby in the box on booklet page 7; then help him write the animal's name on the line. Also have him write his name on the booklet cover. Next, instruct the child to cut out his booklet pages and puzzle pieces. Have him glue the two puzzle pieces for each animal on the appropriate page. Finally, have the child sequence and staple his pages behind his cover. Invite each student to share his booklet with a partner.

Play this animal sounds game to extend the activity. Assign each of several students a different mother animal role. Secretly assign each remaining student the role of a baby belonging to one of the mothers. Then have each mother use the appropriate animal sound to call her babies to her.

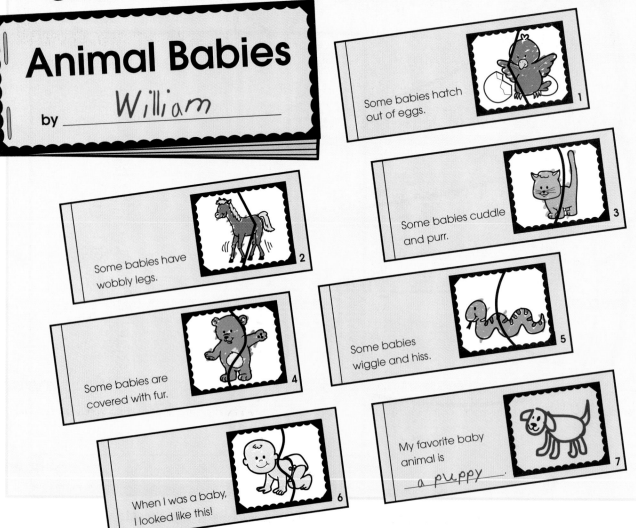

Animal Babies

by _William_

Some babies hatch out of eggs. 1

Some babies have wobbly legs. 2

Some babies cuddle and purr. 3

Some babies are covered with fur. 4

Some babies wiggle and hiss. 5

When I was a baby, I looked like this! 6

My favorite baby animal is _a puppy_ 7

Animal Babies

by _____

©2000 The Education Center, Inc. • *I Can Make It! I Can Read It!* • *Spring* • TEC3514

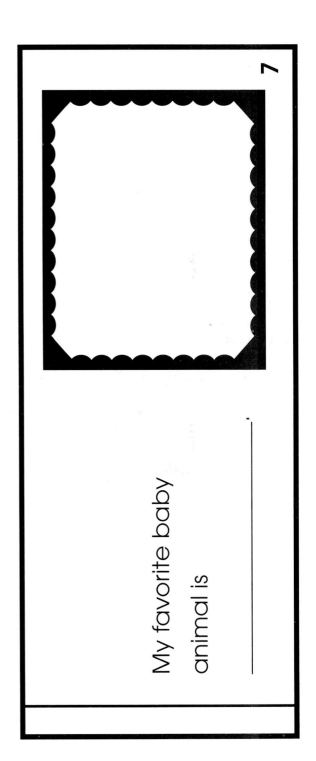

7

My favorite baby
animal is _____

Some babies hatch
out of eggs.

1

Some babies have
wobbly legs.

2

Some babies cuddle
and purr.

3

Some babies are
covered with fur.

4

Some babies
wiggle and hiss.

5

When I was a baby,
I looked like this!

6

Animal Puzzle Patterns
Use with "Animal Babies" on page 54.

THIS IS A BUTTERFLY

Flutter through the pages of these booklets to follow the development of a butterfly. For each child, cut two 5" x 7½" sheets of blue construction paper to use as booklet covers. Then copy pages 60–62 on white construction paper to make a class supply. Ask each child to cut out her booklet pages and patterns. Then have her follow the directions below to complete each page. Afterward, help her sequence her pages and then staple them between the covers. Invite small groups of students to read their booklets with you. Then encourage each child to take her booklet home to share with her family.

PAGE-DECORATING INSTRUCTIONS:

Front Cover: Write your name on the butterfly cutout. Use light crayon colors to decorate the butterfly; then glue it onto a blue cover.

Page 1: Color the leaf green. Use a cotton swab dipped in white paint to dab a small egg onto the leaf.

Page 2: Fingerprint a different paint color on each caterpillar segment. After the paint dries, draw a face on the caterpillar.

Page 3: Color the branch and leaves. Cotton-paint the chrysalis brown.

Page 4: Glue the chrysalis cutout to the page where indicated. After the glue dries, color the chrysalis brown. Then fold it back to create a wing for the butterfly. Color the butterfly.

> Extend this activity by reading aloud Eric Carle's *The Very Hungry Caterpillar* (Philomel Books).

This Is a Butterfly by Abbie

This is the egg. 1

This is the caterpillar. 2

This is the chrysalis. 3

This is the time to wake up. Hello, butterfly! 4

This Is a Butterfly

by _____

chrysalis

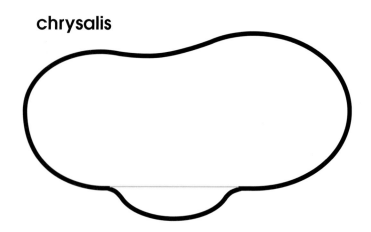

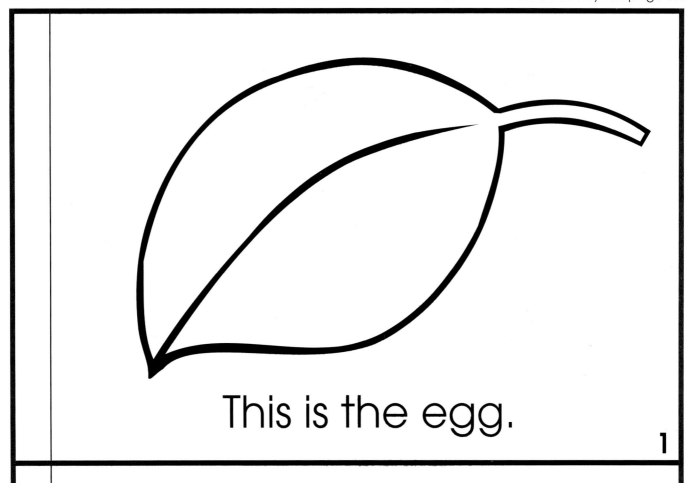

This is the egg.

1

This is the caterpillar.

2

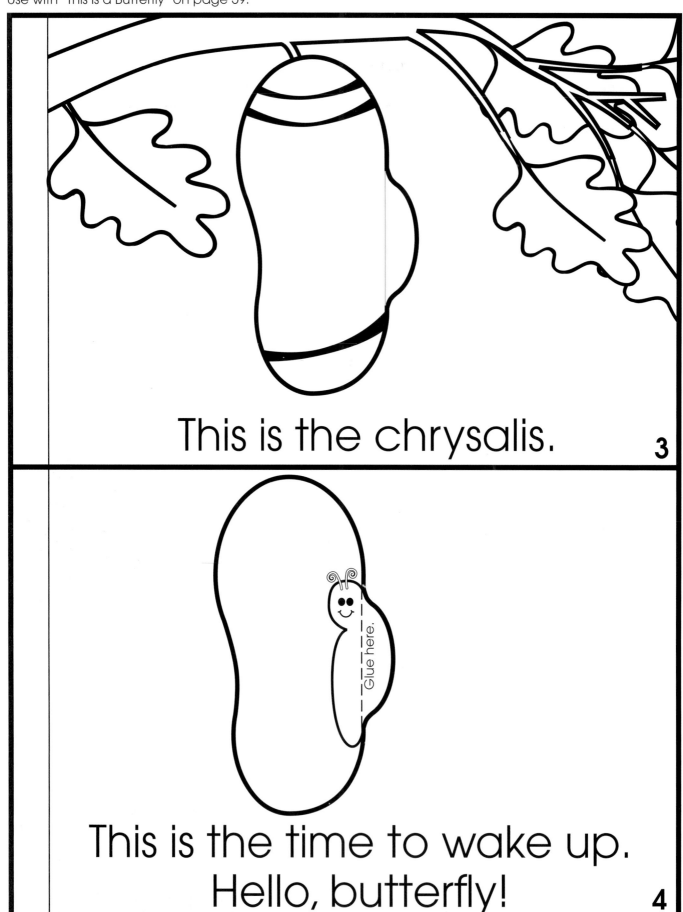

This is the chrysalis.

3

Glue here.

This is the time to wake up.
Hello, butterfly!

4

THE GARDEN PARTY

Flowery text and characters sprout from the pages of these lively booklets! For each child, gather two 9" x 6" sheets of construction paper—one green and one blue—and six 9" x 4" sheets of brown construction paper. Then copy pages 64–66 on white construction paper to make a class supply. To begin, each child colors five wide craft sticks green. He colors each flower as follows: the rose red, the daisy white (with a yellow center), the pansy purple, the daffodil yellow, and the tulip pink. Then he colors the butterfly and his booklet cover and pages. Afterward, the child cuts out each piece.

To make his booklet, each child fringes the top two inches of the green paper, glues his title page to it, and writes his name on the line. Then he glues a booklet page to each sheet of brown paper. Next, the child glues *only* the center of the butterfly to the blue paper. He draws antennae on his butterfly; then he folds its wings so that it appears to be flying. The child staples his sequenced pages between the covers. To make each flower, the child glues a flower cutout to a craft stick. Finally, he glues each flower to the back of the page labeled with its name (as shown), making sure that the flowers are seen over the top of the cover in this order: rose, daisy, pansy, daffodil, and tulip. Conduct a few choral readings of the completed booklets with your class; then send youngsters home to share these delightful booklets with their families.

To extend this activity, have each child cut out pictures of flowers from gardening magazines and catalogs. Ask him to glue each cutout to a large flower shape of the same color.

The Garden Party
by Jessie

Down in the garden
On a warm spring day,
The flowers had a party.
Let's see who came to play.   1

Hello, red rose.
Who invited you?
A fresh white daisy...
That's who!   2

Hello, white daisy.
Who invited you?
A perky purple pansy...
That's who!   3

Hello, purple pansy.
Who invited you?
A sunny yellow daffodil...
That's who!   4

Hello, yellow daffodil.
Who invited you?
A pretty pink tulip...
That's who!   5

Hello, pink tulip.
Who invited you?
A flutter of a butterfly...
That's who!   6

63

Booklet Cover and Pages
Use with "The Garden Party" on page 63.

The Garden Party

by _____

Down in the garden
On a warm spring day,
The flowers had a party.
Let's see who came to play.

1

Hello, red rose.
Who invited you?
A fresh white daisy…
That's who!

2

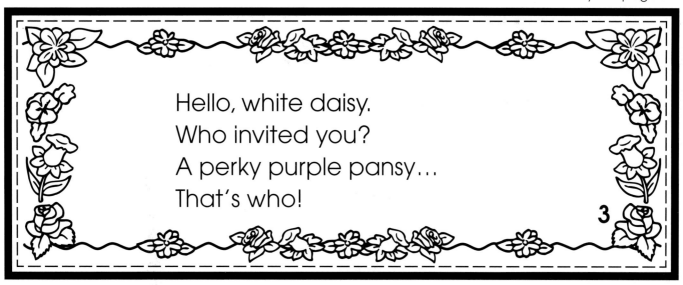

Hello, white daisy.
Who invited you?
A perky purple pansy...
That's who!

3

Hello, purple pansy.
Who invited you?
A sunny yellow daffodil...
That's who!

4

Hello, yellow daffodil.
Who invited you?
A pretty pink tulip...
That's who!

5

Booklet Page and Patterns

Use with "The Garden Party" on page 63.

Hello, pink tulip.
Who invited you?
A flutter of a butterfly…
That's who!

6

butterfly   **daffodil**   **tulip**

rose   **pansy**   **daisy**

MOTHER

Help each youngster spell out her love for a very special person with this booklet. To begin, cut out two 5" x 10" sheets of pink construction paper for each child. Then copy pages 68–71 on white paper to make a class supply. Have each child cut out her booklet cover, pages, and pattern; then instruct her to complete each page following the directions below. Afterward, help her sequence her pages and then staple them between the booklet covers. Encourage each child to read her keepsake booklet to her mom on Mother's Day.

PAGE-DECORATING INSTRUCTIONS:

Cover: Write your name on the line. Glue the cutout to a sheet of pink paper. Glue tissue paper flowers around the border.

Page 1: Make a red thumbprint heart on the page as shown.

Page 2: Use a cotton swab and blue paint to print teardrops on the page; then glue on a small piece of facial tissue.

Page 3: Glue a feather to the page.

Page 4: Affix smiley-face stickers to the page.

Page 5: Color the badge cutout. Glue two short lengths of ribbon to the back of the badge; then glue the badge to the page.

Page 6: Draw a picture of your mother.

Extend this activity by helping each child write out an acrostic for her own name. Have the child glue her picture to the page; then invite her to present it to her mother.

Mother
by Shannon

1 **M** is for the **many** things she does for me each day.

2 **O** is for the special **one** who wipes my tears away.

3 **T** is for the **tickles** and for the good **times** that we share.

4 **H** is for the **happy** smiles that show me that she cares.

5 **E** is for **each** time she helps me do my best.

6 **R** WHEW! After all she does, she's **ready** for a **rest!**

Booklet Cover and Page
Use with "Mother" on page 67.

R

After all she does, she's **ready** for a **rest!**

6

Mother

by _____

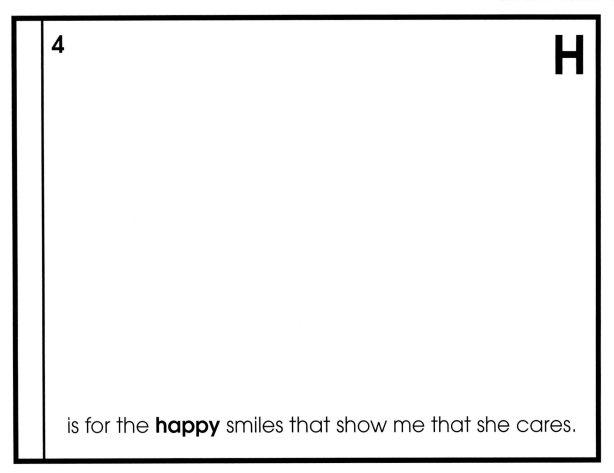

4

H

is for the **happy** smiles that show me that she cares.

M

1

is for the **many** things she does for me each day.

3

T

is for the **tickles** and the good **times**
that we share.

2

O

is for the special **one** who
wipes my tears away.

E

5

is for **each** time she helps me do my best.

badge

SNACK IN A SACK

These mouthwatering booklets are filled with nutritious ingredients and a tasty text. To prepare, gather a class supply of paper lunch bags and sesame seeds. For each child, copy page 73 on a light color of construction paper and page 76 on light brown construction paper. Make a class supply of each of the booklet pages and patterns (pages 74–75) on construction paper as follows: booklet page 1 on yellow, booklet page 2 on medium brown, booklet page 3 and the pickle patterns on green, and the tomato pattern on red. Then have each child cut out his booklet cover, pages, and patterns.

To make a booklet jacket, each child folds down the top 2½" of his bag. He glues his title and verse cutouts to the front of the bag as shown; then he writes his name on the line. To make the booklet, each child sequences booklet pages 1–4 with the top edges together. He tops the pages with the cover and then staples them together. He glues his tomato and pickles on the cover to resemble a face. Then he adds sesame seeds to the cover to complete his booklet. After the glue dries, have each child insert his booklet into his bag; then invite him to tote his snack home in a sack to share some nutritious reading with his family.

> To extend this activity, send home a note to request that parents help their child list all the foods that he eats on an appointed day. Then, in class, help each child find his listed foods on the food pyramid.

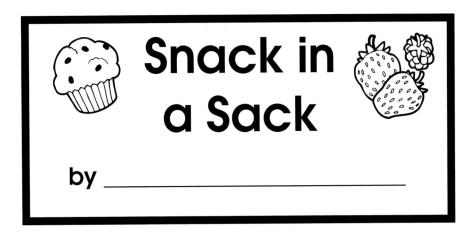

Snack in
a Sack

by _____

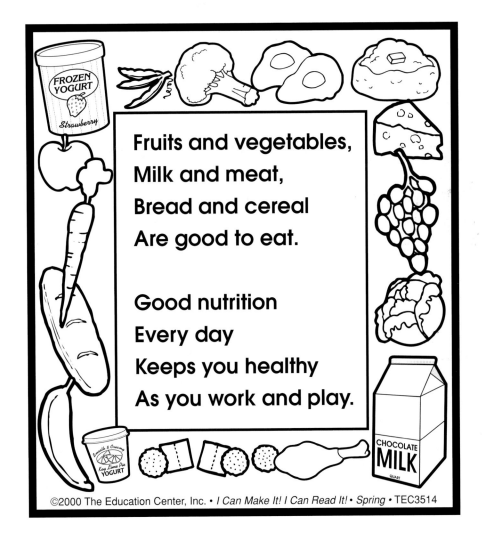

Fruits and vegetables,
Milk and meat,
Bread and cereal
Are good to eat.

Good nutrition
Every day
Keeps you healthy
As you work and play.

©2000 The Education Center, Inc. • *I Can Make It! I Can Read It!* • *Spring* • TEC3514

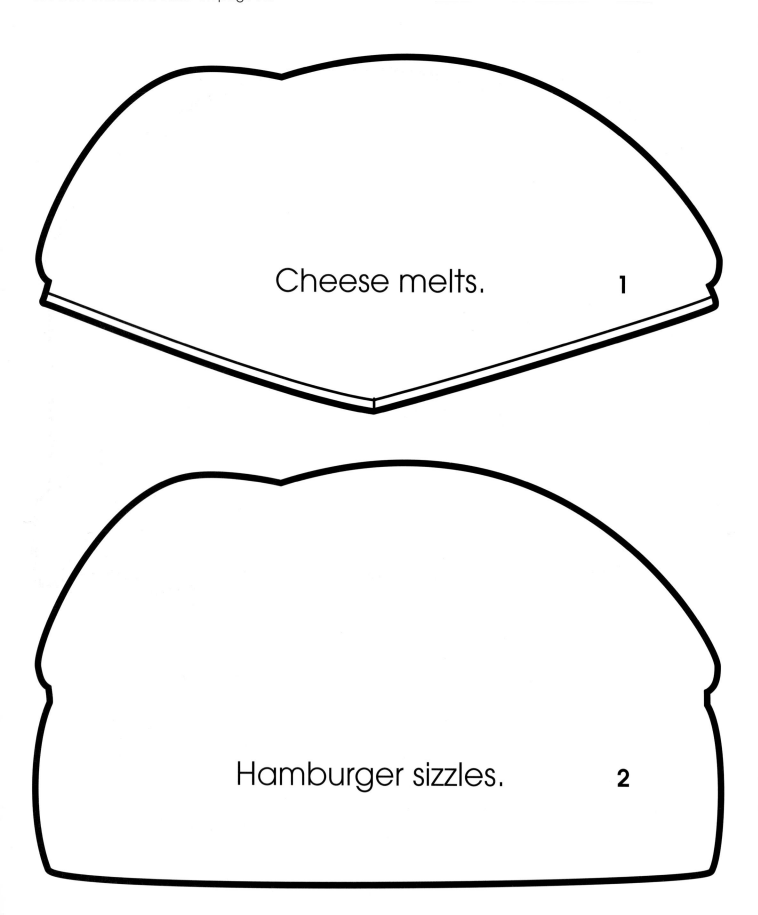

Cheese melts.

1

Hamburger sizzles.

2

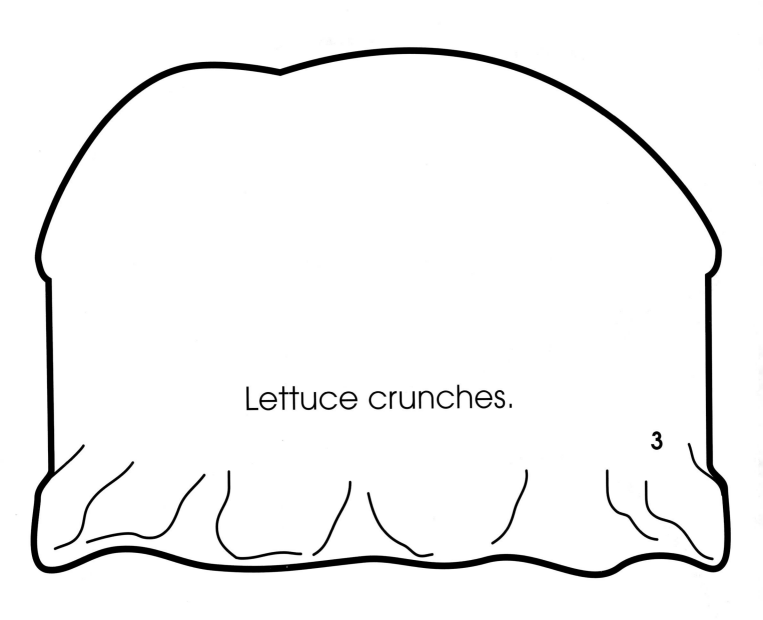

Lettuce crunches.

3

pickles

tomato

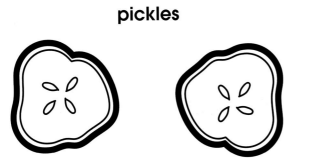

Booklet Cover and Page

Use with "Snack in a Sack" on page 72.

cover

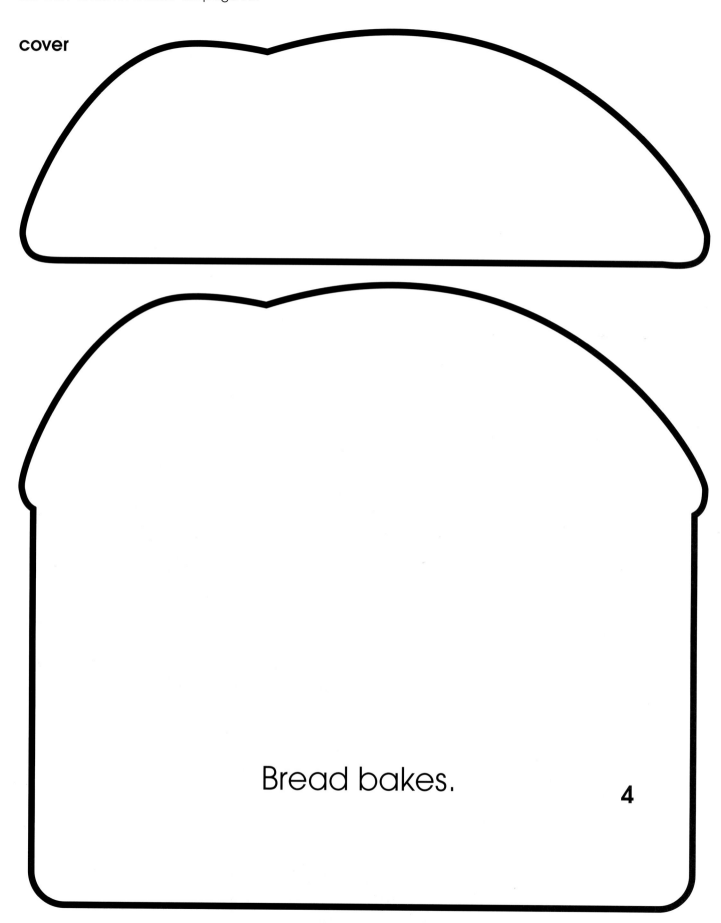

Bread bakes.

4

COLORFUL FEATHERS

Perky birds dressed in vivid feathers hop across the pages of this colorful, easy-to-make booklet. To begin, copy pages 78–81 on white paper to make a class supply. Also gather craft feathers and a wiggle eye for each student. Ask each child to cut out her booklet cover, pages, and wing pattern. Have her color her cover and the wing cutout to match. Help her glue the wing to the cover where indicated; then have her glue a few feathers onto the wing. Also have her glue a wiggle eye onto the bird. Then ask her to write her name on the line. Direct the child to color the bird on each page to match the text. Then have her cut out each word pattern and glue it to the box labeled with the corresponding word. To complete her booklet, the child sequences her pages behind the cover and then staples them together along the left side. Encourage each of your little bird-watchers to read her booklet often to reinforce color words *and* bird names.

To enhance this activity, provide your color-savvy students with a variety of bird books. Challenge them to find more birds for each color represented in their booklets. Then list each kind of bird on a sheet of construction paper corresponding to the bird's color.

77

Booklet Cover and Page

Use with "Colorful Feathers" on page 77.

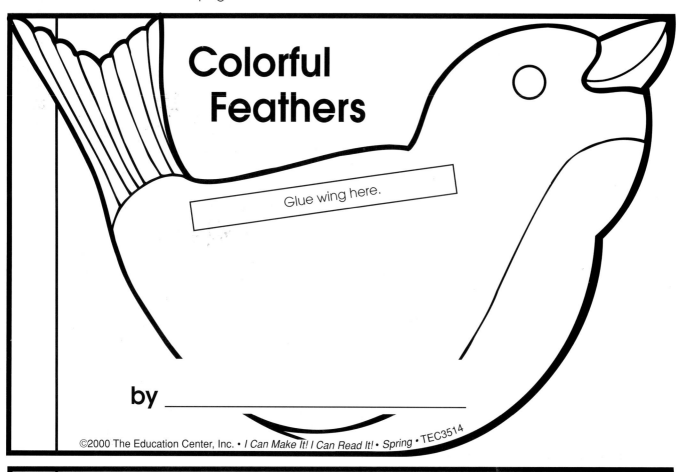

Colorful Feathers

Glue wing here.

by _____

1

goldfinch

Yellow feathers.

2

sparrow

Brown feathers.

3

blue jay

Feathers of **blue.**

4

cardinal

Red feathers.

5

blackbird

Black feathers.

6

parakeet

Green feathers, too!

wing

words

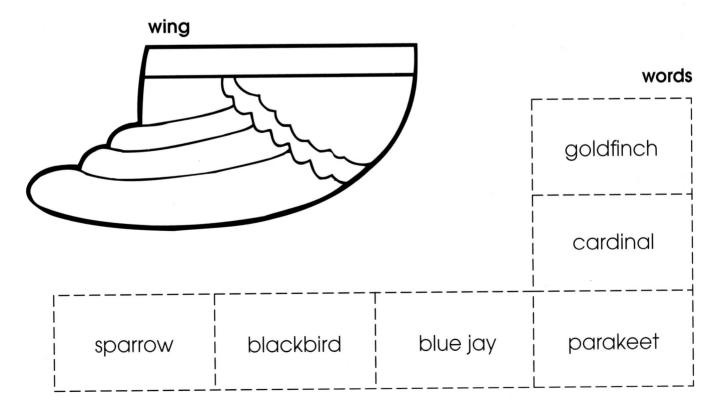

goldfinch

cardinal

sparrow

blackbird

blue jay

parakeet

LITTLE BEE BUZZES

Youngsters will be as busy as bees in a hive when they make these fold-out booklets. To prepare, make a class supply of pages 83–86 on white paper. Also supply each child with two wiggle eyes (optional) and a craft stick. Then have each child color and cut out his booklet pages and patterns. Ask him to draw a self-portrait on booklet page 6, adding wiggle eyes to his picture if desired; then have him write his name on the cover. Direct the child to glue the booklet pages together where indicated, using the symbol guides to match the pages. Then have him glue each positional word cutout to the corresponding page. To make the manipulative puppet, have the child glue the bee cutout to the end of a craft stick. Then help him glue the hive to the cover where indicated to create a pocket for the puppet. After his pages are completed, have each child accordion-fold his booklet so that the cover is on top. To use, have the child remove the puppet from the pocket; then have him move his bee along the dotted line as he reads his booklet, unfolding it one page at a time.

Extend the use of the bee puppet with this adapted version of Simon Says. Simply have each child point his bee to each named body part when the command follows the phrase "Little Bee says…"

82

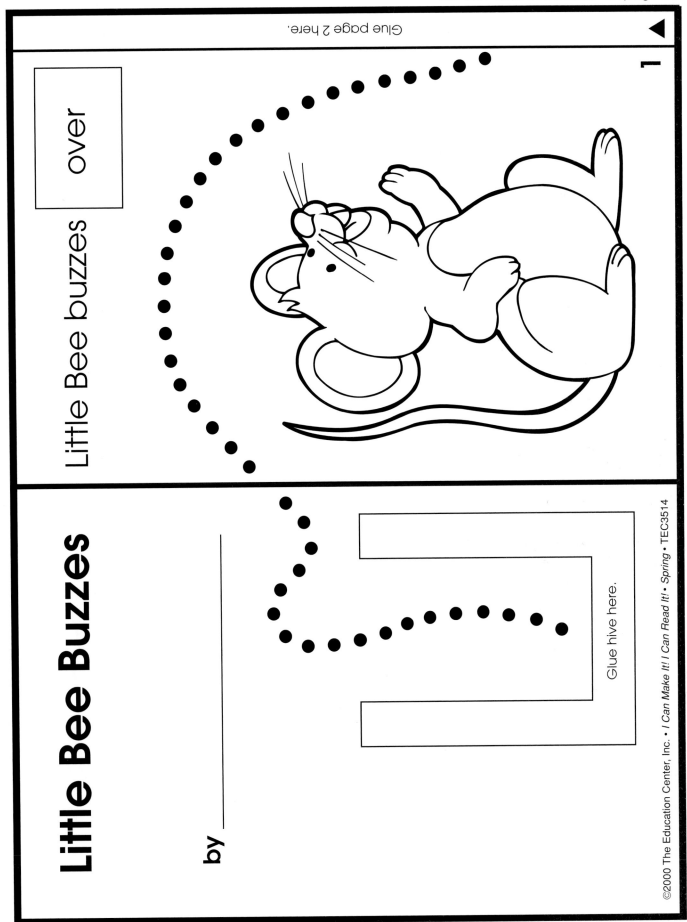

Glue page 2 here.

1

Little Bee buzzes over

Little Bee Buzzes

by _____

Glue hive here.

Booklet Pages

Use with "Little Bee Buzzes" on page 82.

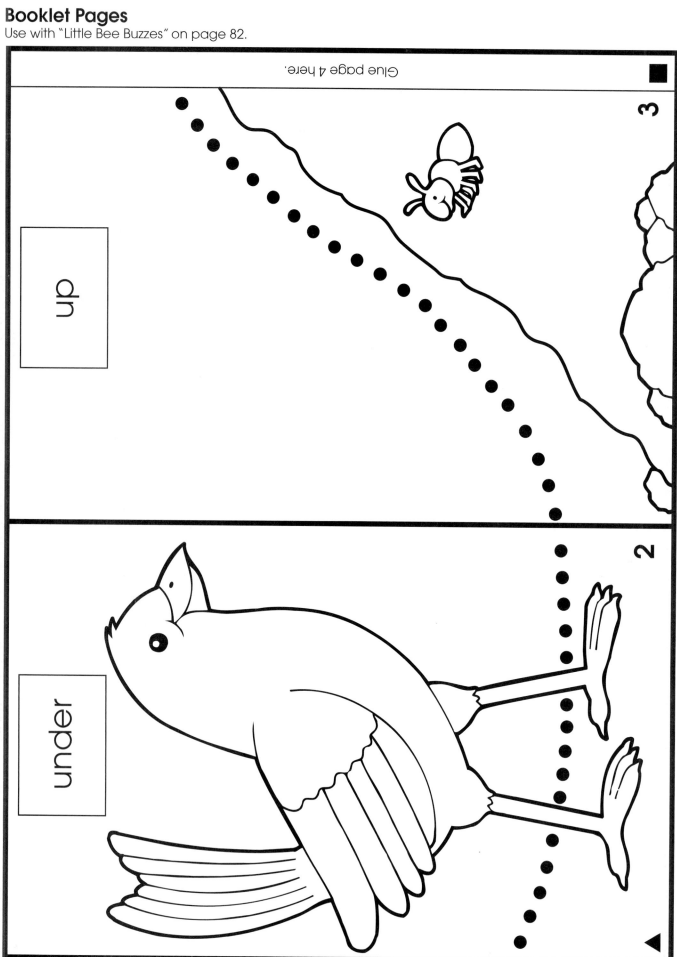

Glue page 4 here.

3

up

2

under

Glue page 6 here.

5

on

4

down

Booklet Page and Patterns

Use with "Little Bee Buzzes" on page 82.

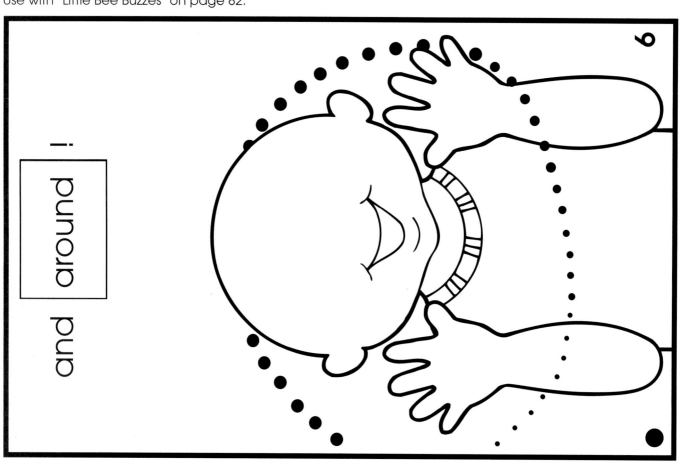

and | around | !

6

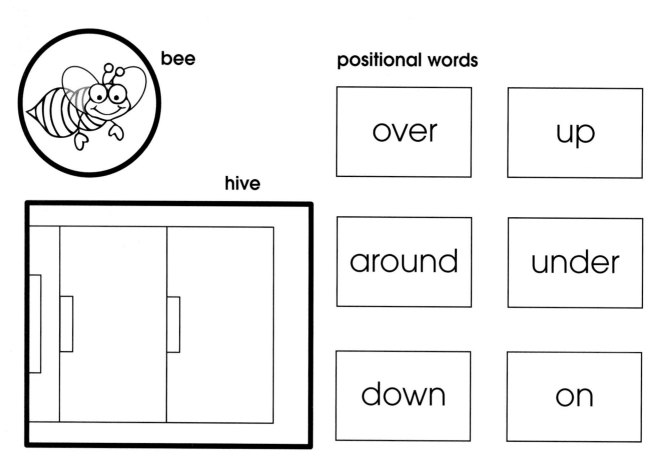

bee

hive

positional words

over	up
around	under
down	on

STRAWBERRY SUE

Send youngsters down to the strawberry patch to pick some friends with which to share this "berry" cute booklet! For each child, gather two five-inch and two seven-inch lengths of green pipe cleaner and four individually wrapped strawberry candies. Then copy the booklet cover and booklet page 7 (page 88) on pink paper and the strawberry cap on green paper to make a class supply. Also copy pages 89–91 on white paper for each child. Then list each child's name on chart paper. To make a booklet, each child cuts out her pages and the cap pattern. She writes her name on the cover and glues the green cap on it. Then she writes a classmate's name on the line on each page, referring to the chart for the correct spelling. She colors each picture to resemble the named child.

Laminate the cover and booklet page 7 for each child; then invite her to assemble her booklet. To do this, each child punches holes where indicated on page 7. She attaches a five-inch pipe cleaner to each top hole and a seven-inch pipe cleaner to each bottom hole. Next, she twists the loose end of each pipe cleaner around a piece of candy as shown. To curl the pipe cleaner arms and legs, the child wraps each one around a pencil and then removes the pencil. Finally, she staples her sequenced pages to the cover. Invite each child to share her booklet with the classmates named in her text.

> To extend this activity, have each child write her name with glue on a sentence strip and then sprinkle strawberry gelatin powder on the glue. Display these "scent-sational" name cards at your students' nose level. Smells great!

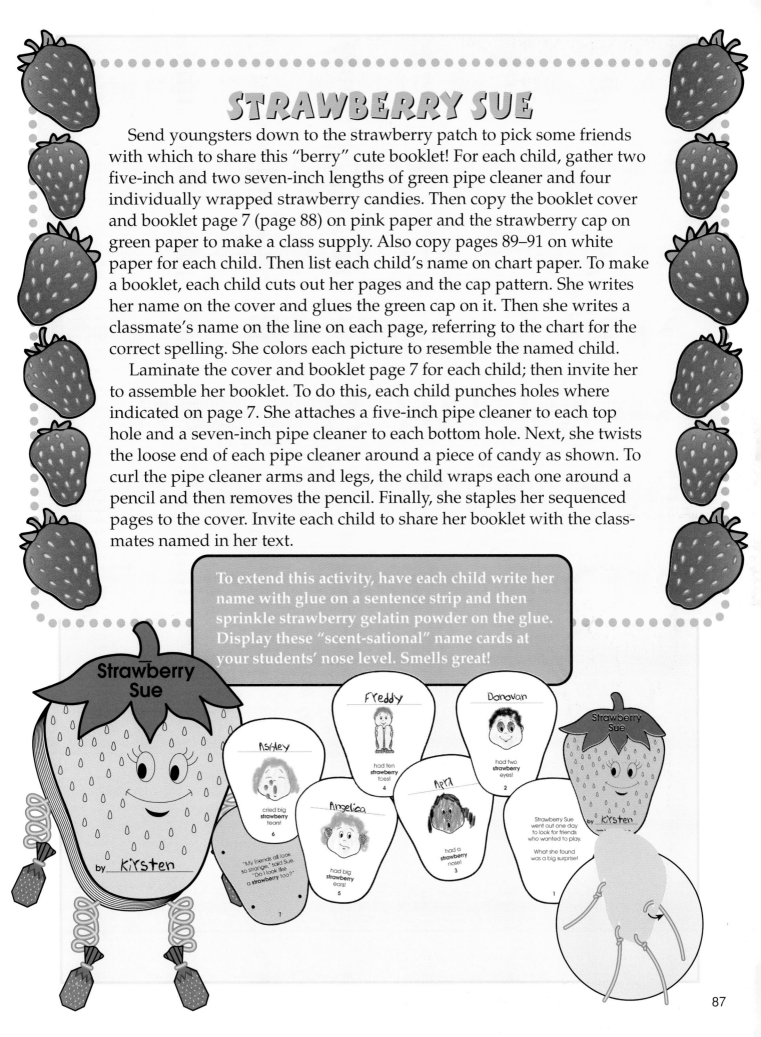

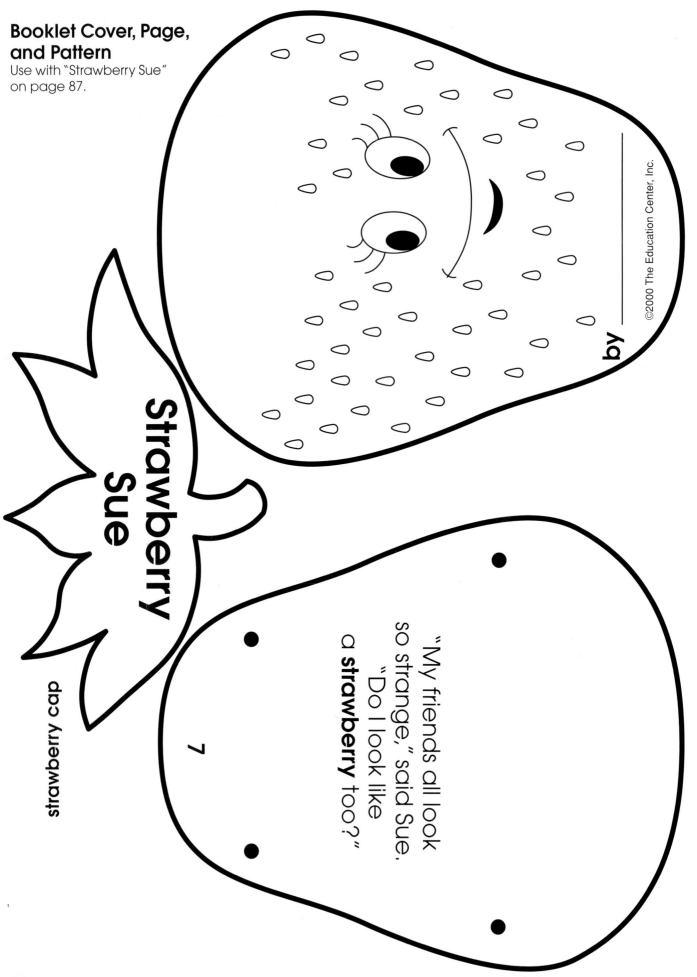

Strawberry Sue

by

©2000 The Education Center, Inc.

strawberry cap

"My friends all look so strange," said Sue. "Do I look like a **strawberry** too?"

7

Strawberry Sue
went out one day
to look for friends
who wanted to play.

What she found
was a big surprise!

1

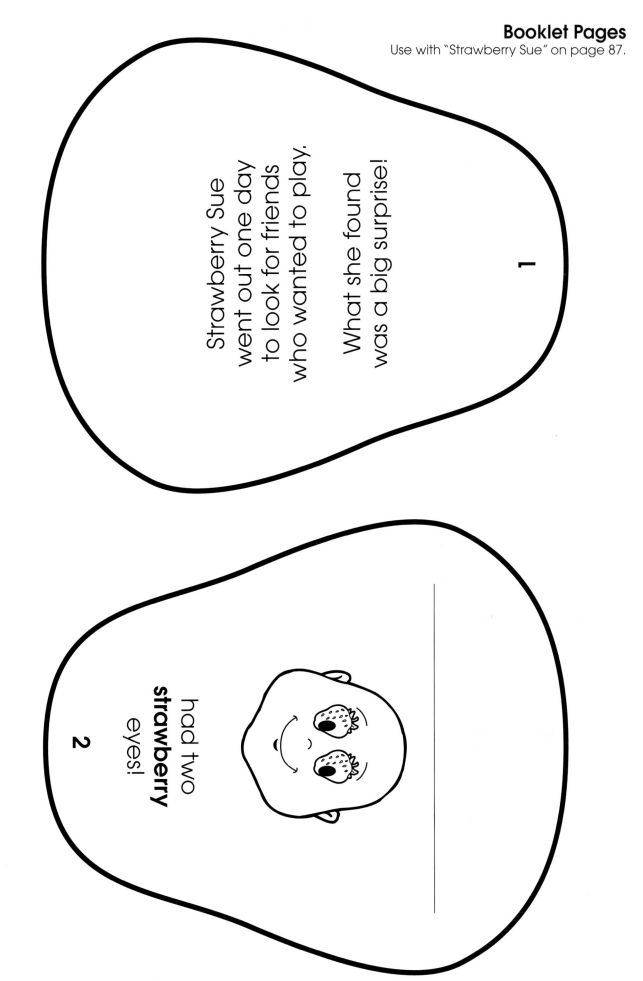

had two
strawberry
eyes!

2

had a **strawberry** nose!

3

had ten **strawberry** toes!

4

had big **strawberry** ears!

5

cried big **strawberry** tears!

6

ANIMALS BUILD

Animals build structures for many reasons, such as to hide from enemies, to catch food, to protect themselves from heat or cold, or to raise their young. Invite young-sters to build this booklet to discover some of the interesting structures made by ani-mals. To begin, duplicate pages 93–96 on white construction paper to make a class supply. Then have each child cut out his pages and decorate them according to the directions below. Afterward, have him sequence his booklet pages and then staple them together along the left edge. Invite each child to share his booklet with the class and then take it home to share with his family.

PAGE-DECORATING INSTRUCTIONS:

Cover: Write your name on the line. Color the picture.

Page 1: Color the picture. Dip a plastic fork in brown paint; then use it to print sticks on the lodge.

Page 2: Color the picture. Glue brown crinkle strips, raffia, or Spanish moss on the nest.

Page 3: Color the spider black. Trace the web with a gray crayon, pressing firmly as you draw. Then paint the picture with water-thinned black paint.

Page 4: Color the picture. Glue coffee grounds on it to represent dirt.

Page 5: Color the inside of the den black. Glue cotton snow around the outside of the den.

Page 6: Color the tortoise. Sponge-paint the ground brown.

> Extend this activity by sending a copy of the parent note (page 96) home with each child. When students return their notes, invite them to share their discoveries with the class.

A beaver builds a **lodge.** 1

A bird builds a **nest.** 2

A spider builds a **web,** and then it stops to rest. 3

A rabbit digs a **warren.** 4

A polar bear digs a **den.** 5

Animals Build

by _____

Kevin

A tortoise digs a **burrow,** and then it crawls right in! 6

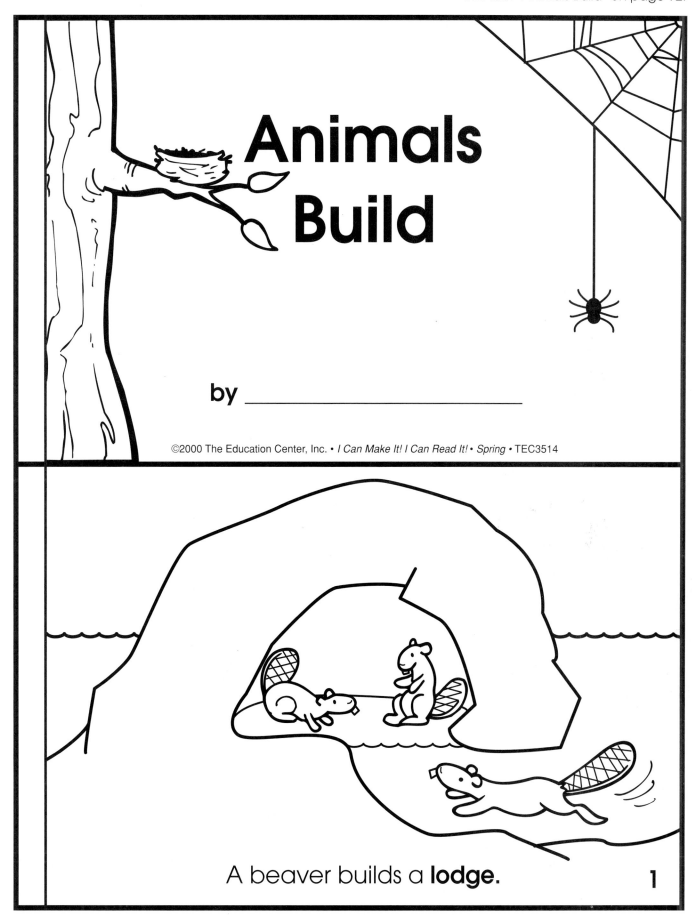

Animals
Build

by _____

©2000 The Education Center, Inc. • *I Can Make It! I Can Read It!* • *Spring* • TEC3514

A beaver builds a **lodge.**

1

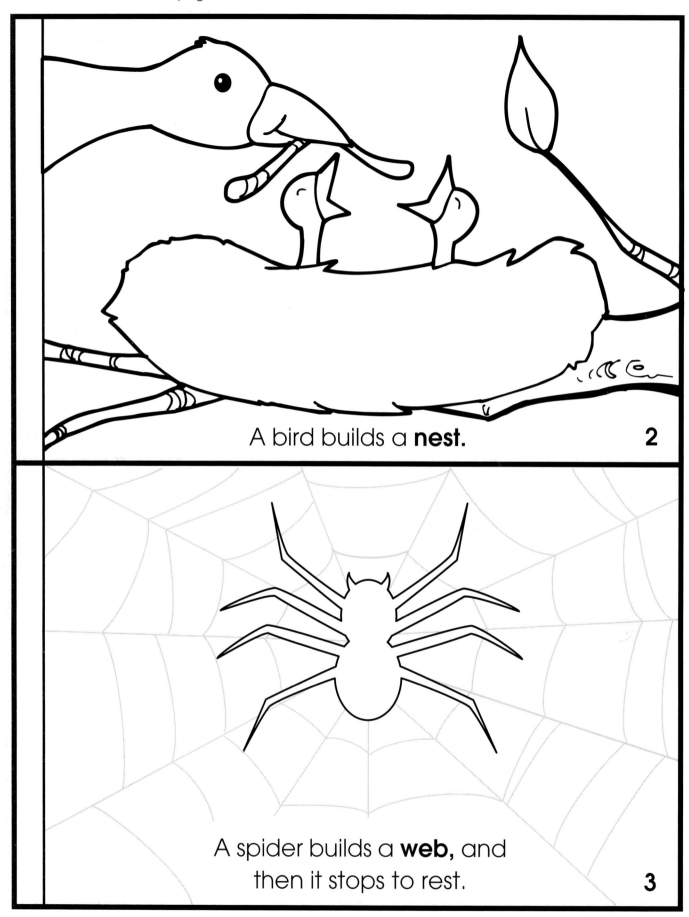

A bird builds a **nest.**

2

A spider builds a **web,** and
then it stops to rest.

3

A rabbit digs a **warren.** 4

A polar bear digs a **den.** 5

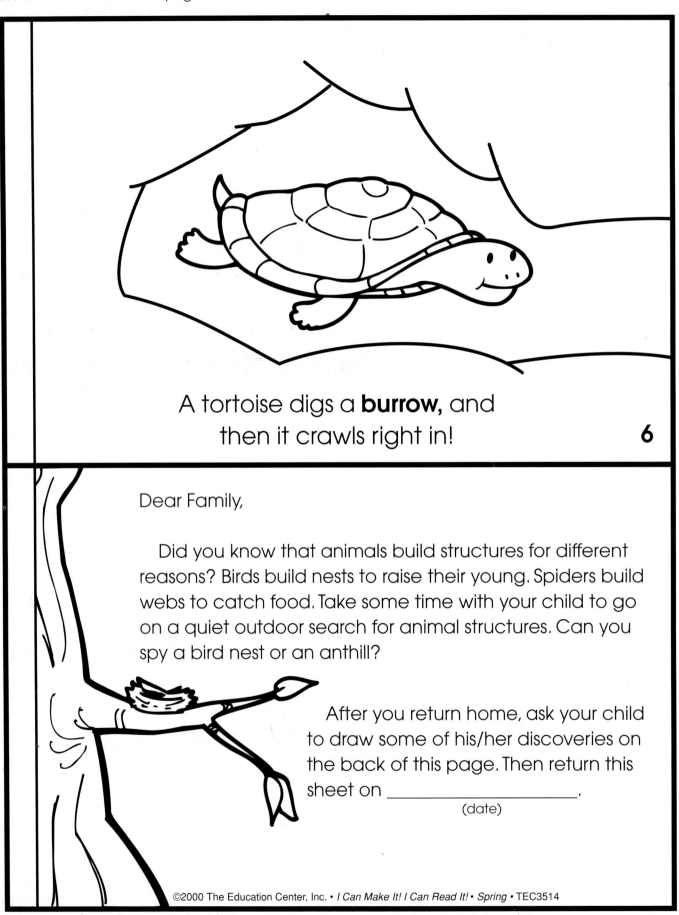

A tortoise digs a **burrow,** and
then it crawls right in!

6

Dear Family,

Did you know that animals build structures for different reasons? Birds build nests to raise their young. Spiders build webs to catch food. Take some time with your child to go on a quiet outdoor search for animal structures. Can you spy a bird nest or an anthill?

After you return home, ask your child to draw some of his/her discoveries on the back of this page. Then return this sheet on _____.

(date)